Alice Walsh

Something's Wrong with Kyla's Mother

Something's Wrong with Kyla's Mother

Alice Walsh

NIMBUS PUBLISHING LTD

Nimbus Publishing Limited
P.O. Box 9301, Station A
Halifax, N.S.
B3K 5N5

Design Editor: Kathy Kaulbach
Project Editor: Alexa Thompson
Cover Illustration: Etta Moffatt

Nimbus Publishing Limited gratefully acknowledges the support of the Maritime Council of Premiers and the Department of Communications. The author thanks the Nova Scotia Department of Tourism and Culture for their financial support.

Canadian Cataloguing in Publication Data

Walsh, Alice.
Something's wrong with Kyla's mother
(Newwaves)
ISBN 1-55109-032-5
I. Title. II. Series.

PS8595.A57S66 1992   jC813'.54   C92-098697-8
PZ7.W35So 1992

Printed and bound in Canada

For Sheila, Joy, and Rosemary

Contents

1
The Dream

It was happening again. I was trapped inside a room with no doors or windows. The grey, brick walls were closing around me. I couldn't breathe. Desperately, I ran around the room, clawing at the brick, but could find no way out. I screamed, a long, drawn out scream that echoed in the blackness.

"Kyla? Kyla, wake up." I felt my father's hand on my shoulder. My sister Julie was beside him looking concerned and puzzled. "It's just a bad dream," I heard him tell her. "Go back to bed."

A cold sweat trickled down my forehead and I could feel the nylon of my nightie sticking to my back. The digital clock on my bureau said 7:02, almost time to get up. I was glad I didn't have to close my eyes again.

I was still shaking an hour later when I went

downstairs to find Julie with Mom's apron on. She was frying sausage and pancakes for breakfast while Dad poured my little sister, Bunny, a glass of milk.

"Feeling better?" he asked me.

I nodded, taking my place at the table.

"Mom is not feeling well," he said.

My mother is always sick it seems. She suffers from headaches, backaches, stomach upsets, and she cries a lot.

I hoped she wasn't still upset about the note I had brought home from school last week. The teachers were always giving me notes to give her. *Dear Mrs. Masters: Kyla could be a good student if only she paid attention in class. She tends to daydream....* I try hard not to get into trouble, but somehow I always manage to mess up.

"Why can't you be more like your sister?" is my mother's favourite line. Julie is perfect. She comes home from school every evening and does the housework. She does the cooking, the shopping, and takes care of Bunny. Who can compete with that?

Grandma once said that Julie and I were no more like sisters than swans were like crows. We don't even look alike. Julie is very pretty with black hair that hangs halfway down her back. She has beautiful green eyes with long, dark lashes and teeth that are straight and even. I, on the other hand, have red, fuzzy hair that won't stay flat no matter how many times I wet it down. My nose is wide and sprinkled with freckles. I am a little overweight and it looks as if I will have a double chin some day. To make matters worst, I may have to get braces next year.

Unlike me, Julie manages to get good grades. "You must be very proud of your daughter," the teachers always say to Dad. "Her grades are excellent and she's such a responsible child."

"She's quite a girl," Daddy will say, hugging her close.

Whenever they carry on like that, I feel like handing out barf bags.

My sister Bunny is a different story. She spends hours in her room playing with dolls and looking at picture books. Although she is nearly six-years-old, Bunny sometimes talks like a baby. "K-ah, me slee your room?"

"Bunny, you're not a baby, talk right," Julie tells her.

Whenever anyone is cross with Bunny, her dark eyes fill with tears, and she hides her face in the sofa or in her pillow.

"Kyla?" Dad touched my shoulder. I jumped.

"Kyla, you're not with us this morning." He was holding a large platter filled with pancakes and sausages.

"Huh?"

"Would you like something to eat? This is my final offer." He smiled at me and the pupils of his grey eyes became larger, like jellyfish spreading their tentacles.

"Sorry, Dad," I mumbled, and helped myself to three pancakes and four sausages. The smell of maple syrup mingled with fried sausage made me feel a whole lot better. Quickly, I dug my fork into a pancake. I love food. It is a joke in my family about how much I can eat. I just eat and eat as if I can't stop. Sometimes when I'm in school I keep thinking about the snack I have for recess.

"Kyla, take time to chew your food." Julie frowned at me from across the table. Although she is only three and a half years older, she sometimes acts as if she is my mother.

I ignored her. "When is Mom going back to

work?" I asked Dad.

"Your mother is tired. She needs a rest."

"Mommy threw up on the bathroom floor," Bunny said, her eyes wide as she looked from Dad to Julie, and then at me.

"Don't worry about it, Honey," Dad said. "Eat your pancakes or you'll be late for school."

I went into the livingroom to look for the TV guide. I had circled the programs I wanted to watch when I got home from school. *Growing Pains* is my favourite. I sometimes wish my family was like the family on this program. This is how families are supposed to be.

"Want a ride, Kyla?" my father asked, as he helped Bunny put on her coat.

"I'll walk," I told him. We live only a few blocks from the school. Besides, I didn't want anyone to see the snack I had packed for recess—four cookies, an apple, a banana, a roll, and a can of soda.

Just as I was getting ready to leave, Mom came downstairs wearing Dad's bathrobe. Strands of blonde hair hung limply around her pale face and her red-rimmed eyes were sunk into dark hollows.

"Mom, the teacher says...."

"Not now, dear." She made an impatient gesture

with her hand. I watched as she gulped down a large glass of orange juice without taking her mouth away from the glass. With shaking hands, she refilled the glass, then sat down at the kitchen table and lit a cigarette.

I thought of the mother on "Growing Pains," and the mothers of my friends at school.

There is something very wrong with *my* mother.

2
A Thief At School

I arrived at school just minutes before the bell rang. Lorna Lindsay ran to meet me, her face flushed with excitement. "Guess what?" she said, holding tightly to her little brother's hand. There was a large sore on her chin and the blouse she wore had a large stain in front. Lorna's hair is always lank and greasy and she often comes to school wearing clothes that are dirty or don't fit properly.

"Someone stole Andrea Franklin's camera," she said, breathlessly.

"Who?"

"Dunno," she shrugged. "It was taken from her desk."

Andrea was standing at the far corner of the school yard talking to a circle of wide-eyed, inquisitive girls. I walked over to them and Lorna followed. Her little brother let go of her hand to wipe his nose on his sleeve.

"At least it was insured," I heard Andrea say as I got closer. Andrea moved here a couple of months ago, and we are both members of the school's photography club. Since the school has a darkroom, we are often given photography assignments. Twice a month, Mr. Bryce, our instructor, takes us on field trips to the Public Gardens or Point Pleasant Park. Andrea is very nice and I hope someday she will be my friend.

The bell rang before I had a chance to talk to her. On the way to my class I thought of how that camera had been the envy of the sixth grade.

The first period was Social Studies. Perhaps if it had been some other subject I might not have gotten into trouble, but Social Studies is so boring I can't keep my mind on it. This morning we were learning about the Acadians.

"Although the Acadians tried to remain neutral in the Anglo-French conflict," Ms. Connors was saying, "they suffered greatly at the hands of the British soldiers."

While she talked I daydreamed about Kirk Cameron. In my dream he had come to Halifax

and had picked me, out of all the girls at school, to
go out to dinner with him. I had lost ten pounds,
Dad had bought me a very expensive dress, and I
had even found a hair dresser who was able to get
all the kinks out of my hair.

"Kyla?" I don't know how long Ms. Connors
had been standing by my desk, arms folded across
her chest, but I was angry at her for interrupting
my dream. "Kyla, I asked you a question," she
said.

"Huh?"

She spoke very slowly as if I was a very young
child. "Which poem by Henry Wadsworth
Longfellow is about the suffering of Acadian
exiles?"

I squirmed in my desk, my face hot with
embarrassment, and shook my head. Ms. Connors
looked annoyed but didn't say anything. I really
tried to pay attention after that, but soon found
myself dreaming about Kirk Cameron again. When
the bell rang for recess, I was asked to stay behind.

"What were we talking about in class this
morning, Kyla?" Ms. Connors asked after everyone
else had left the room.

"The Acadians."

"And?"

"I don't know," I stammered, and looked at the floor.

"You didn't hear a word I said, did you, Kyla?"

I wasn't surprised when she sent me to Mr. Tibbets' office.

Mr. T., as we like to call him, is the principal, and I have been sent to his office more than once. Just last week I was sent for eating bits of my snack during class. A couple of times he had asked to see Mom and Dad, either because I wasn't paying attention or because I was falling behind in my schoolwork.

Before I left the classroom I grabbed two cookies from my desk, which I ate in the bathroom before going downstairs to Mr. T.'s office.

"You can go in now, Kyla." Helen Clark, the secretary, smiled at me as I walked into the office. She is always friendly and speaks to me whenever she meets me in the hallway. Her son, Kevin, has recently joined the photography club.

"What can I do for you today, Kyla?" Mr. T. asked. He was looking at some files and didn't even bother to look up at me. I hate it when he asks what he can do for me, as if I had asked to see him.

I didn't even want to be there.

"Ms. Connors sent me," I told him.

"And why do you think Ms. Connors sent you to me, Kyla?"

"I don't know, she didn't say."

"I understand you're not paying attention. According to your teacher, you tend to daydream." He looked up from the file and gestured for me to sit down. "What do you think about, Kyla?" He peered at me through bushy eyebrows.

"Nothing."

"Nothing, eh?" He leaned back in his chair making church steeples out of his short, fat fingers and pressing them against his double chin. "This is the third time this month you've been to see me. Is something bothering you?"

"No."

"How old are you now?"

"Almost twelve," I mumbled.

"It's not boys, is it?" He smiled slowly, revealing teeth that were large and yellow.

I blushed and looked straight ahead at the filing cabinet that had Adams-Day stamped across the front.

"How is your mother?" He knew my mother

had taken time off work because she was sick.

"Fine, she was doing laundry when I left this morning."

Mr. T. sighed and got up from his chair. "Your sister is doing so well in junior high. I really don't know what your problem is, but a lot of kids would consider themselves lucky to have all the advantages you do."

I left his office feeling guilty. I should be more grateful for all the things I had; my father is a well known lawyer and we live in a nice house on a nice street. I have my own room, my own television, and my own stereo. I'm not poor like Lorna Lindsay who wears secondhand clothes given to her by the church.

"Something wrong?" Helen asked when she saw me. I must have looked the way I felt.

For a moment I wanted to cling to her and say, "Yes, yes, something is wrong. Please help me." But that was silly. I was lucky, everyone said so.

"Kyla, if there is anything I can do for you, please let me know."

I nodded, not knowing what she could possibly do, and wondering why she was being so nice to me.

The bell rang ending recess and the corridor became filled with activity as kids filed in from outside, taking off jackets and sweaters and making their way to their classrooms.

I was standing alone in the hallway feeling resentful about having to go to the principal's office, when Andrea came by. "Kyla, where were you all morning?"

"I was helping Helen in the office—you know, stapling sheets of paper, photocopying, that sort of stuff." Then, to quickly change the subject, I added, "Sorry to hear about your camera."

"I guess there's not much I can do, but I feel really bad about it."

I nodded. "I just loved all the different lenses that went with it. Were they stolen as well?"

"Yeah," Andrea sighed, as we walked to our next class.

After we had all settled down, Mr. T. made an announcement over the P.A. system. He got straight to the point. "We have a thief in our school," he said. "A number of things have been stolen from the classrooms, both here and at the junior high." Everyone in our class looked at Andrea. "So far, a camera, a tape and a sweater are missing. Until we find out who is behind this, don't leave your things unattended. If you have any idea who the thief is come and talk to me or to one of your teachers. You may not want to tell on your friends or classmates, but it is very important for us all that the thief should be caught."

On the way home for lunch, there was a great deal of excited talk about the stolen camera. "I bet I know who did it," said Megan Kushner. She looked very smug with her new hair cut and her expensive jacket.

Everyone stopped talking and waited expectantly.

"Lorna Lindsay."

3
What's Wrong Mom?

As I turned into our street, I thought about what Megan had said about Lorna. It made me really angry. I knew Lorna had wanted to join the photography club but her mother could not afford to buy her a camera and, besides, she had to take care of her younger brother and sister everyday after school. Still, that was no reason to accuse anyone of stealing.

I was mad at myself for not sticking up for Lorna because I like her and want to be her friend. The problem is the other girls don't like Lorna, and if they know I spend time with her, they probably won't want to be friends with me. I often go to visit her without telling Julie or the other girls, but I hate sneaking around like that. Frustrated, I kicked a rock and hurt my toe.

As I got closer to home, knots began forming in

the pit of my stomach the way they always do. I never know what Mom will be doing. I hesitated at the kitchen door, my heart pounding. She was sitting at the kitchen table still in Dad's bathrobe, with an opened bottle of gin standing next to an overflowing ashtray. I could tell she had been crying; her eyes were so swollen they looked like half-cooked mussels.

"What's the matter with you?" she demanded as soon as she saw me.

"Mom, what's wrong?" I cried, although I knew right away the school had called. Ms. Connors had warned me that if I continued to daydream in class she would have to let my parents know. I really didn't think she would do it, but she had.

"My other children never give me a bit of trouble," she slurred. "You … you.…" She cradled her head in her arms, breaking into fresh tears.

At that moment, Julie burst through the door. "Mom!" She let go of Bunny's hand, rushed to my mother's side, and put both hands on her arms. "What's wrong, Mom?" she asked as she shot me a dirty look. "Come upstairs and lie down."

I watched helplessly as my sister took my mother's arm and pulled her gently to her feet.

"Is Mommy gonna be sick again?" Bunny tugged at my elbow.

"I don't know," I told her. I had stopped making up excuses for my mother a long time ago.

"I want Daddy," she whined. When she took off her coat, I noticed that her red corduroy pants were wet.

"Don't you ever go to the bathroom?" My voice was a lot sharper than I intended, but Bunny often wet her pants or her bed.

"Where's my Daddy?" Bunny's brown eyes started to fill up with tears.

Immediately I felt sorry. She looked so helpless standing there in the middle of the kitchen, her face thin and pale, her bottom lip quivering.

"Come on, I'll help you change." I hated seeing her upset.

Julie came downstairs and, without saying a word, went into the kitchen to prepare lunch. While she opened a can of soup, I emptied ashtrays. The plant on the windowsill in the kitchen was dead, so I threw it in the garbage. I felt sad when I remembered how beautiful the plant used to be with its pink and white blossoms. There are always dead plants around our house.

My stomach was still in knots when I went to the table for lunch. I couldn't swallow, and the vegetable in the soup tasted like lumps of sawdust in my mouth.

"Did you hear about Andrea's camera?" I asked Julie to break the silence in the room. I was aware of the humming of the refrigerator, the ticking of the clock and Bunny's spoon scraping on the bottom of her bowl.

Julie nodded.

"Megan Kushner says it was Lorna Lindsay who took it, but I'm sure it wasn't."

Julie's eyes opened wide. She opened her mouth slightly, but closed it again. Then she looked at me thoughtfully.

"Kyla, I really don't think you should hang out with kids like Lorna."

"Why not?"

"Well, because … well, she's so …" Julie wrinkled her nose, "… so shabby."

"Oh, *please*." I rolled my eyes toward the ceiling, even though it is true that everything about Lorna is shabby. Her family lives in a run down rooming house where they have to go all the way to the third floor to use a bathroom they share with all the other tenants. Lorna doesn't have a father and her mother works as a waitress at *Madame Benoit's* restaurant.

Still, she is the only one of my friends I feel relaxed with, and she doesn't seem to care about anything my mother does. She always makes a fuss about how big our house is and exclaims over all the nice things we have.

Julie doesn't have any friends. There used to be a boy—Paul—I think his name was—who used to stop by the house to study with Julie. But since Mom stopped working, Julie doesn't bring anyone around anymore. I wonder what it would be like to have no friends.

"I just remembered," I said, jumping to my feet. "Ms. Stevens wants us to bring in pictures of our family for health class—something to do with genetics and physical traits." The pictures really didn't have to be in until Monday, but I was glad to have an excuse to leave the table.

The photograph albums which hadn't been taken down in a long time were stacked neatly on a shelf in the livingroom. I spread them out on the hardwood floor, carefully turning the cellophane pages. The first album is filled with pictures of

Mom and Dad's wedding, with Dad dressed in a white tuxedo and Mom wearing a long, white dress with a veil. They look like the mannequins on display in the window at Eatons. I can't remember my mother smiling the way she does in those photographs.

Most of the pictures were taken when Julie was younger. There are pictures of Julie in pigtails, Julie with her front teeth missing, Julie feeding the ducks in the Public Gardens. Except for the occasional school picture, there aren't very many pictures of me. I couldn't find any pictures of Mom and me together. Perhaps I was adopted, I thought; that would explain why I was so different. There weren't any photographs of Bunny and Mom together either. In fact, the only photographs of Mom were those taken when Julie was very young.

"It's the stress of having *two* small children to care for," I once heard Grandma tell my dad. I had often wondered what she meant. Perhaps if I hadn't been born things would have been all right with my family.

The ringing of the telephone interrupted my thoughts.

"Kyla?" It was Dinah Taylor, a girl in my class. "I'm having a party," she announced, "and I want you to come."

"Great!" I told her. "When? Never mind, don't say another word. I want you to tell me all about it on the way to school."

"I'll meet you in five minutes," Dinah said, out of breath.

"Great!" I put the albums carelessly back on the shelf, stuffed four cookies in my jacket pocket and ran out of the house.

4
The Field trip

Dinah waved excitedly when she saw me. She looked elegant in a bright red dress with a wide black belt. She wears her thick black hair in an elaborate pattern of tiny braids decorated with brightly colored glass beads. She told me it takes hours to get her hair that way.

Although Dinah and I are friends, we are very different. Dinah takes things much too seriously. She wants to be a lawyer when she grows up, and once, when she went with me to my father's office, she asked him all kinds of questions about his job.

"Do you really want to be a lawyer?" I had asked her, when we were on the elevator going down from his office.

"What I would really like to be is a judge," she replied, "or, perhaps I could go into politics. Maybe I'll be the first black Prime Minister."

"I'll be happy if I can get through sixth grade," I told her. In some ways Dinah reminds me of Julie.

Today, though, all she talked about was the party. "It's to be girls only," she said, "my mother's idea. I think she's afraid I'll invite Kevin Clark again."

I smiled as I remembered Dinah's last party. The lights had gone out suddenly and everyone had gathered in the livingroom. We were sitting in the dark when we heard weird noises coming from upstairs. Then we saw this figure in white walking slowly down the stairs. It was Kevin with a sheet wrapped around him. He was chasing a couple of kids around the livingroom when someone tripped and knocked over a lamp. Dinah's mother had been very upset about that.

Dinah talked about the party all week. "It's going to be a sleep over," she told me on Thursday, when classes were over and we were at the photography club.

"Who's going to be there?"

"Well, I've already asked you so I thought I'd invite Megan, Andrea, and maybe Cindy Howe."

"Girls, pay attention," Mr. Bryce looked at us, his forehead creased in a frown. "It's such a nice day today, I think we'll head for the Public Gardens," he said. "I'll be talking about the difference between natural light and artificial light. It might be a good idea to bring along your tripods."

"I forgot mine," Dinah said. "Can I borrow one from the school?"

"Who else doesn't have one?" Mr. Bryce looked around the room, as a few hands shot up.

"I'll see if I have enough," he said. "As you know, some of our photography equipment has been stolen. May I remind you not to leave lenses and cameras around the school."

"Light is the photographer's medium," Mr. Bryce explained on the way to the Gardens. We tried to pay attention, but most of us were distracted by Kevin. For the first couple of blocks he walked on his hands and people stopped to stare at him.

"He's such a ham," Dinah whispered. "I wish he could come to the party."

When a lady in a tight skirt and high-heeled shoes walked by, Kevin imitated her movements exactly. Everyone laughed.

"Kevin, grow up," Mr. Bryce hissed, his lower jaw moving up and down under his beard. I could tell he was getting angry. "I expect a group of sixth graders to be more mature when I take them out in public."

"Yes, Sir." Kevin jumped to mock attention.

Mr. Bryce shot him an angry look, but continued with the lesson. "Sunlight," he said, stopping to look upward, "is a highly unpredictable source of light."

We all tried to keep straight faces when, moments later Kevin, behind Mr. Bryce's back, peered up at the sun with a puzzled look on his face. All afternoon he was the centre of attention. We took pictures of him standing on his head, with his fingers up his nose and his toe in his ear.

Before leaving the Gardens, Mr. Bryce asked us to sit in a circle. "Does anyone here want to enter a photo contest?" he inquired.

Immediately Kevin's two hands shot up. "I do, I do. Me too, please."

Mr. Bryce didn't even look at him. "The contest is for students in grades five to nine, and there will be cash prizes. The winning photographs will be displayed at Atlantic Mall."

"When do the pictures have to be in?" someone asked.

"Oh, not until January, so you'll have plenty of time."

"The judging will take place some time in March. Also, I want everyone to go through their collections this week to find photographs for our open house which is just a couple of weeks away."

Twice a year our school has an open house during school hours. Parents sometimes sit at the back of the classroom while classes are in session. Displays of students' projects are set up for them to look at.

"I would like to have at least two of everyone's very best photographs," Mr. Bryce said.

I had dozens of good photographs, but there was no doubt in my mind which one I would use. Julie, Bunny and I had been cleaning out the attic one evening when Bunny had fallen asleep. Her head was resting on an old trunk, and she was holding a rag doll she had found in one of the boxes. I had taken a great shot using the late evening sun which poured through the small window. Bunny's sleeping face was lighted up while everything else was in shadow. Mr. Bryce had raved about the picture for weeks.

"Can we use the same photograph in the contest and in the open house?" I asked.

"Sure can," Mr. Bryce replied.

On the way back to school, I was walking ahead of the others when Dinah Taylor caught up with me. "Kyla, remember that half roll of film I shot with your camera?"

"Yes, I developed that roll last week while you were sick. The negatives are at home."

"Good, I'll stop by and get them," she said.

"Sure." I didn't sound very convincing but was unable to come up with any excuse why she couldn't. What if my mother was drunk, crying, or had passed out on the floor? What if she said things to insult Dinah? Dinah would tell her parents and I wouldn't be allowed to go to her party. She would tell Megan who would make fun of me the way she had of Lorna. I was filled with anxiety.

Megan's father, the Reverend Kushner, had no use for drunks. I had gone to church with Megan a couple of times and on one occasion he had stated that drunkeness was a sin.

"They call it a disease," he said with disgust, "but it's a sin and there's no getting around it." He had looked directly down at me sitting in the front pew with Megan and her mother. I felt sure that somehow he must know about Mom's drinking.

Someone put a hand on my shoulder and I

jumped. "Relax."

Mr. Bryce was smiling at me. "You're going to enter the contest aren't you, Kyla? I think you have a very good chance of winning."

"Yes," I told him. "I'm going to enter the picture of my little sister asleep in the attic."

He wrinkled his forehead, then stroked his grey beard the way he always did when he was trying to remember something.

"Ah, yes," he said after a moment. "Good choice."

"You almost ready, Kyla?" Dinah was standing by the school door waiting for me.

On the way home I prayed, "Please, God, don't let my mother be drunk." But just in case God wasn't listening, I crossed my fingers and rehearsed what I would say to Dinah.

5
Charming Man; Needs TLC

Mom was taking a batch of cookies from the oven when I opened the door and the smell of chocolate permeated the kitchen.

"Hello," she greeted us cheerfully. I wanted to hug her.

"Mom, this is Dinah Taylor."

"Dinah Taylor? Now, how do I know that name?" She looked down at the floor as if the brown tiles would give her the answer.

"I'm the girl who's having the party," Dinah told her.

"Party?"

"Oh, Mom, I forgot to tell you. Dinah is having a slumber party in a couple of weeks." The truth is I hadn't told my mother about the party because it had been one of her bad days when Dinah had asked me. She never remembers the next day anyway, so what's the use?

"What a good idea, a slumber party." My mother clasped her hands together. "Why don't you have a slumber party, Kyla? We could have one for your twelfth birthday."

"My birthday is not until December," I reminded her.

"Well, Dear, December is only a couple of months away."

"But it's so close to Christmas," I protested.

"You could have a Christmas and birthday party all in one," Dinah said. Her dark eyes were eager as she looked first at me, then at my mother. "I'll help you get things ready."

Once more I felt my palms go cold and clammy.

"Your Mom's nice," Dinah said later, when we were alone in my room.

"Yes," I agreed. I was so pleased she liked my mother that for the next half hour we played the stereo in my room while I pretended my family was just like any other. It was one of the happiest afternoons of my life.

That evening we ate in the diningroom with Mom at one end of the table and Dad at the other. We had roast chicken and three different kinds of salad. Mom wore the blue dress Dad had given her last Christmas. She had piled her blonde hair on top of her head, and put on some makeup. I had forgotten how pretty my mother really is.

"Wait a minute," I said, before we started eating. "I want to take some pictures."

"Oh, no," my father groaned playfully, but I ran upstairs to get my camera. I placed the camera on a tripod and set the timer so that I could be in the pictures too. By the light of the four candles on the diningroom table, I shot half a roll of film.

"From now on, Kyla, things are going to be different around here," my mother told me, as I helped clear the table.

"From now on, there are going to be cooked meals. I've been putting too much responsibility on you and Julie."

During the days that followed, my mother was like a politician during election time. She made all kinds of promises she couldn't possibly keep. In our house there were always promises. I knew I should never take anything my mother said seriously, but I wished so hard for things to be different.

For a few days it looked as if things really would

change. Dad came home for supper every night instead of staying late at the office as he usually did. Mom took on all kinds of projects. She painted the bathroom, papered the hallway upstairs, made curtains for my bedroom, planted flowers, and talked about finding a new job.

"Aren't you going to go back to work at the hospital?" Julie asked one day, while my mother was looking through the job ads in the daily paper. She had been a hospital lab technician for many years.

"I don't think I'm cut out to be cooped up in a lab all day long," she said. "What I need is a job where I can meet people—some place where I can be my own boss. Real estate seems a good business to go into."

She had set her portable typewriter on a small desk in the corner of the dining room. Everyday she answered job ads.

"I wonder why she wants to change jobs," I heard Julie say to Dad one evening. "It doesn't make sense."

I knew why Mom couldn't go back to the hospital. I had overheard the fight she'd had with Dad the day she quit. My room is next to theirs, and I had awakened to the sound of angry voices. I got out of bed and went and stood by my bedroom door so I could hear better. I didn't like to eavesdrop, but I was scared and I had to know what was going on.

"For Goodness sake, Sylvia," Dad was saying, "mixing up lab samples is very serious. It wouldn't surprise me if this patient brings a law suit against the hospital."

"No one knows it was me." My mother's voice was rising to hysteria. "It could have been any one of us."

"I warned you about going to work when you've been drinking too much the night...." Their bedroom door opened, then slammed. As I crept back to bed, I could hear Mom walking down the hallway to the guest room. It had been a long time before I had been able to get back to sleep.

The next Saturday Mom took me shopping for new school clothes. Although school had started six weeks ago, this was the first chance she'd had to take me out, and I felt happy as we walked into Scotia Square together.

We looked at sweaters, dresses, jeans and shoes.

I was struggling to get into a pair of jeans when I saw my mother give me a strange look. "Kyla, you've really been putting on the pounds. What have you been eating?"

I hung my head and bit my lower lip. Swallowing hard, I tried to keep the tears from flowing. I felt ashamed and the warm feeling I'd had was gone. All I wanted to do was leave the store and go home.

Since my mother had stopped drinking, I was constantly being drilled by Julie and Dad about what I should and should not do. "Don't you ever do anything to upset her again, Kyla," Julie warned. "Mom is doing so well." Sometimes I felt as if the whole future and happiness of my family depended on how I behaved. In a way my mother's sobriety was almost as hard on me as her drinking.

Julie was always on my case and it was wearing me out. I was nervous and jumpy, and there were circles under my eyes from lack of sleep. "Did you get that book report done?" she asked one morning when Mom had left early to go to the dentist. "We don't want the school to call and get her upset again."

"Shut up!" I screamed at her. "Just shut up and leave me alone." I sat on the stairs, buried my face in my knees, and cried.

That afternoon, instead of going home, I went to Lorna's house. She hadn't been to school that day and was excited to see me. Her mother often keeps her home to take care of her younger brothers and sisters.

"Come in," she said, grabbing my arm and pulling me inside.

I looked around the small room in disgust. Dishes were piled high on the tiny cupboard; plates encrusted with food were left on the table; dirty mugs, greasy bowls and unwashed pots and pans lined the small counter. The room reeked of soiled diapers and dirty laundry.

Lorna's baby brother crawled around the floor, his feet and hands red from the cold. He wasn't wearing a diaper, there were sores on his legs and his nose was running.

"I wanna go outdoors," Lorna's three-year-old sister, April, kept repeating.

"Shut up, April, before I belt you one." Lorna held up her hand to the whining child.

"Let's make some phone calls," she said to me, ignoring the baby who had reached inside the overflowing garbage can and was playing with an empty soup tin.

"Phone calls?" I was puzzled. "Why?"

"Kevin," she said, then giggled as she picked up the phone and dialed. "Is your fridge running?" she asked. "Then you'd better run and catch it." She quickly hung up the receiver, laughing at her own joke.

"It was Kevin," she said.

She dialed a couple of other numbers but, getting no answers, put down the phone. "I know what we can do." She went out into the hallway, to pick up the newspaper that was left by someone's door.

"Lorna, what are you doing with that? It's not yours."

"Oh, I'll put it back later." She brought the paper inside, then opened it to the classified section. "Let's write to some of these people."

"What people?"

"Listen to this." She began to read. *"Lady 45, great figure, would like to meet gentleman 45 to 50."*

"Look at this one," I said, reading the ad below it. *"Charming man in late forties, very affectionate and needs TLC. Would like to meet woman 25 to 35. Looking for a permanent relationship. Send photograph."*

"I like that one," Lorna said. "Let's write to the charming man in his late forties."

"But we have to send a photograph."

"Perhaps you could send a picture of your mother?" Lorna suggested.

"I know," I told her, "I have a picture of my Aunt Veronica. We can send him that." Aunt Veronica is my father's sister. "She used to be a model and she lives in the United States. She is still very elegant."

"She's old, is she?"

"Very old," I told her, "must be at least thirty-five."

Lorna opened a can of spaghetti, poured it into an unwashed pan and invited me to stay for supper. It didn't look very appetizing and anyhow, I knew my mother would be expecting me. Besides, I wanted to get home so that I could type the letter on Mom's typewriter.

As soon as the dishes were cleared away that evening, I sat down at Mom's desk. One of her letters was still in the machine. A copy of today's newspaper was next to the typewriter. Circled in red was, *Leading real estate firm looking for trainees. Send resumé.* Carefully, I took out Mom's letter and put in a blank sheet of paper.

I typed my address and the date in the right hand corner, just as Ms. Lang, our English teacher had taught us. *Dear charming man*, I began. I sat for fifteen minutes just staring at those three words. *I saw your ad in the newspaper and think you would be a neat person to marry someday.* That sounded stupid, so I crumpled up the letter and began again. Another ten minutes went by and all I had written was *Dear charming man.*

I picked up the letter my mother had written. *To whom it may concern*, she had begun. *I am writing regarding the ad in the October 20 issue of your newspaper. I am a hard worker and like what you have to offer. Enclosed is a personal resumé. If you need to contact me, you may do so by writing to the above address.*

Half an hour later, I had finished my letter. It was almost an exact copy of my mother's letter. The only difference was that my mother had said she was enclosing a resumé, but I had written that I was enclosing a picture of myself. I signed the letter, Maureen O'Riley, using the name of a pen pal I used to write to in Ireland. I typed the envelope and put in the letter and the photo of Aunt Veronica. Then I stuck on a stamp and put the envelope in my schoolbag. I would mail it in the morning.

6
'Kyla, We Have Your Mother Here'

On Thursday afternoon I went into the darkroom to make prints from the roll of film I had taken of my family at the dining room table. As I placed the photographic paper into the developer and watched my mother's smiling face come into focus, there was a tightness in my chest. My eyes filled with tears, and very carefully I wiped them away with my fingertips. I loved my mother so much—could it be my fault she had to drink?

After I had taken all the prints out of the final chemical solution, I looked at my work with pride. The pictures had turned out so well that I made plans to have some of them matted and framed as gifts for my grandparents at Christmas. There was no doubt in my mind that I would use one of them in the open house, maybe in the photography contest as well.

On the way home from school, I showed the pictures to Andrea. "My family," I said proudly.

Andrea studied the photographs carefully. "The lighting is very good," she said. "I've always liked photographs shot by candle light."

"Mr. Bryce says we should try to experiment with different kinds of light."

Andrea nodded. "Dad bought me a roll of infra-red film to take pictures at the Mardi Gras tomorrow night."

"Mardi Gras? Tomorrow night?"

"It's being held on Saturday instead of Hallowe'en night," she explained.

"But aren't you going to Dinah's slumber party?"

"No, we made plans for this a long time ago," Andrea said. "Our whole family is going, and we've had our costumes rented for weeks."

"Oh, that's too bad," I replied, as we stopped in front of my house. "But I'll see you on Monday. Have fun."

"You have fun at the party." Andrea tossed her long blonde hair, then moved her book bag to her other shoulder before moving on.

As I watched her hurry up the street, I felt disappointed that she wouldn't be at the slumber party. Andrea had a way of making people feel at ease, and I enjoyed her company. I knew Lorna wouldn't have been asked instead. Lorna was never invited to parties.

When I opened the door and stepped into the foyer, I could hear the phone ringing. Not bothering to take off my shoes, I dropped my knapsack on the hardwood floor and ran to answer the phone.

"Mr. Masters, please?" said the male voice on line.

"Dad is at work. This is Kyla, his daughter."

"Kyla, this is Steve Restin down here at Restin's Drugstore. We have your mother here. She ... she's passed out. Could you call your dad, Kyla?"

"Passed out?" I could feel my stomach turning over in that old familiar way. A lump came into my throat making it hard for me to talk. I started breathing faster. "I'll call him," I said.

Quickly I hung up, then dialed the number Dad had put by the phone. When I told him what had happened there was a long sigh, then a moment of silence. "Where's Julie?" he said finally.

"She's not home from school yet."

Another sigh. I could imagine him running his hands frantically through his red hair the way he always does when he is upset. "All right, Honey, I'll be right there."

I flew out of the door, then down the street, my heart pounding under my wool sweater. I wanted to keep running, but I stopped when I came to the big sign that said *Restin's*.

I could see Mom sitting in a chair in the middle of the aisle. A group of people had gathered around her, and one of the clerks was holding an ice pack to her head. As I got closer, I heard one woman say, "She's been drinking."

"Loaded drunk," whispered an elegant lady in a fur coat. "Disgusting."

"Mom?" I ran up the aisle knocking several boxes of band aids to the floor. "Mom?" I repeated as I got closer.

She didn't answer. Her eyes were closed, and her head hung down loosely like a newborn infant's.

"My mother hasn't been feeling well lately." I had spoken to the clerk and Mr. Restin, but this statement was meant for the group of curious onlookers. I glanced sideways at the nosey biddy in the fur coat.

"Go away!" I wanted to scream. Why didn't

they leave? I hated them staring at my mother like that. I could just imagine them sitting at the supper table that evening, telling their families about the drunken lady who had passed out in the drugstore.

I was relieved when I saw Dad in the doorway. With both hands shoved into his pockets and his mouth pursed into a grim line, he made his way toward us. I wrapped my arms around him and sobbed. I couldn't help it, and I didn't care that everyone was looking at me. He held me tightly for a brief moment, then let go.

"Where's Julie?" he asked.

I shrugged. "She's probably home by this time."

He shook my mother gently. "We're going home," he told her. Gingerly, he put both his arms around her waist and lifted her from the chair. Her head rolled from side to side and both legs were sprawled under her. One of her high heeled shoes came off and Dad put it into the pocket of his overcoat.

"I can manage," he said crisply, when someone tried to take Mom's arm. Together, we dragged my mother outside to Dad's station wagon which was parked on the street, and got her into the backseat. I got in beside her. A group of school children stopped to stare. They made a straight line on the sidewalk, the way people do when a parade is passing by. I prayed that no one from my class would see us.

On the way home, my mother rested her head in my lap. As the car pulled into the driveway, Julie came running out of the house, her forehead creased with concern. I was beginning to see that look on her face more and more often these days.

The three of us tried to get Mom out of the car, but she pushed us away. Kicking her legs and flinging her arms wildly, she shouted, "No! Don't. Go away."

Across the street, I could see Mrs. Noseworthy and her husband at the kitchen window. They watched as we struggled to get Mom up the veranda steps. On the way into the house, she threw up on Dad's new shoes.

There was no supper that evening. After we had put Mom to bed, Dad went back to the office. Since Bunny was staying at a friend's house, Julie didn't bother to cook.

"I have a lot of homework," she told me, and went upstairs to her room.

After making a sandwich from a leftover can of

meat, I, too, went to my room. I was anxious to start reading a book of ghost stories I had borrowed from the school library. The book was so popular that I'd had to put my name on a waiting list, and I had waited nearly two months before getting it.

I was right in the middle of reading a story about a girl possessed by demons when my mother stumbled across the hallway, and began retching in the bathroom. I set the book aside, put on my earphones, and turned the volume on my stereo up high.

7
A Letter, A Party, and Mardi Gras

The next morning Dad and Julie had already finished breakfast when I came downstairs. The fragrance of bacon and coffee filled the kitchen. Mom was still in bed.

"Would you like some bacon and eggs?" Dad asked.

"No thanks." I reached for the box of cereal in front of me. "This is fine." From the livingroom, I could hear Bunny lisping to her dolls.

"You give me so much trouble. Why can't you be like your sister?" she scolded.

After breakfast I went to the corner store to buy junk food for Dinah's party. I filled my knapsack with pop, potato chips, dip, cookies, nuts and chocolate bars. I love slumber parties because I get to stay away from home. At someone else's house I can relax and not have to worry about my mother.

Sooner or later though, my friends would expect to be invited to my house. This always happened whenever I made a close friend. I still remember Susie Eastman from fourth grade. We were best friends until her mother asked my mother if Susie could stay overnight with us while she was away. Mom got drunk and Susie became scared. She called her mother long distance to come and get her. After that, Susie wasn't allowed to play with me. I tried not to think about inviting friends home. I was determined to have a good time at Dinah's slumber party.

As I ran up the front steps, I noticed flyers and envelopes sticking out of the mailbox. In all the confusion yesterday, I had forgotten to check the mail. Reaching inside the brass box, I pulled out a stack of magazines, bills and junk mail. I looked through each item carefully until I found a narrow white envelope addressed to Maureen O'Riley.

Everyday for two weeks, I had been looking for this letter; it was a reply to the letter Lorna and I had sent to the newspaper. I tore it open eagerly; inside there was a letter and a photograph.

I held the photograph in my hand and stared incredulously.

"Mr. T.," I whispered. I knew it was a picture taken by the school photographer because it had the same backdrop as the pictures he had taken of Julie, Bunny and me. I looked around nervously, wondering if someone was playing a joke on me.

The handwriting was small, neat and easy to read. *Dear Maureen*, he wrote, *I can't tell you how pleased I am to hear from you. Thank you for your lovely photograph.*

Let me tell you a little bit about myself. I am 49 years old and have never been married. I am the principal of an elementary school in Halifax. As I mentioned in the classified, I am looking for a permanent relationship. I want a wife and perhaps, someday, children. However, we can talk about this when we meet.

Would you like to have dinner with me at the Candlelight Restaurant on Tuesday, Oct. 31, at 7:30 P.M.? I'll be looking forward to meeting you. The letter was signed, *Yours Sincerely, Henry Tibbets.*

Mr T.! Mr. T. was the charming man in his late forties. I couldn't wait to show the letter to the girls at the party. I knew they would all just die.

That evening I put on my best jeans and new blue sweater. Then I tried to get my frizzy hair to stay flat. It still stuck up even after I had used half a can of mousse. Finally, I decided to put it all back in the fancy banana clip Julie gave me, but even then, bits of hair stuck out at the ends.

At 7:10, I arrived at Dinah's house to find the other girls already dancing to the music of a rock video on a small television set. There were just the four of us—myself, Dinah, Megan, and Cindy from the other grade six class.

Dinah was about to show the video *Adventures in Babysitting*, when I showed her the letter.

"Check this out," I said.

As Dinah read the letter, her forehead wrinkled. "I don't get it," she said. The others looked at me blankly. Quickly, I explained about the ad in the classifieds.

"Get outa town." Dinah burst out laughing.

"I don't believe it. Old Mr. T. on the loose," said Cindy.

"So, are you going to go and meet him?" Megan asked.

"Are you kidding? Of course not. If he knew I wrote that letter, he'd probably kill me."

"We can all go," Megan suggested.

"You must be crazy," I replied.

"Well, it's on Hallowe'en night, isn't it? We

could wear our costumes, then stand outside the restaurant to see if he shows up. It's a public place. We can go there any time we want."

Megan looked eagerly from one person to another.

"Let's do it," Dinah said. "Tuesday night at 7:30, right?"

We all agreed.

It was nearly 9:30 before we started watching the movie. Every inch of the Taylor's spacious family room was covered with sleeping bags, bowls of potato chips, dip, peanuts, crackers and plates of donuts oozing with jelly.

When the movie was nearly over, Dinah's mother opened the door. "Dinah, dear, we're going to bed now. Is there anything we can get you?"

"No, Mom, we're just fine."

"Don't stay up too late."

As soon as the door had closed behind her, Cindy unrolled her sleeping bag. "Got it," she said. In her hands she held half a pint of rum. Everyone clapped, even Megan, but at the sight of the bottle, I felt knots forming in the pit of my stomach. My palms grew cold and sweaty.

"And I brought these," Cindy held up styrofoam cups and several cans of coke. She poured rum and coke into each cup, then handed them around. I took one, but I had no intention of drinking it.

"A toast," Dinah said, "to Mr. T. May he marry, have children, then retire." Everyone laughed.

Slowly I lifted the cup to my lips, and touched the drink with the tip of my tongue. The stuff smelled and tasted terrible. I couldn't figure out why Mom liked it.

Thoughts about my mother made me angry. I cringed when I remembered her falling down in the drugstore yesterday. How much longer could I keep my friends from knowing my mother was a drunk?

Without meaning to, I took a swallow of the rum and cola. "This stuff is not for me," I thought, as I coughed. I sipped it slowly. After a moment, I began to like the way it burned, then warmed, my insides. The stuff wasn't that bad.

"Let's get dressed," Dinah said after awhile.

"What?"

"We're going downtown to the Mardi Gras."

"Now?" I asked. It was almost midnight, and I wanted to stay and finish the rest of my chips and dip. Reluctantly, I put on my coat and followed the others.

By the time we reached Argyle Street, the Mardi

Gras was in full swing. "Fifty thousand people are expected here tonight," Dinah said. "Isn't it exciting?"

Dinah was right. Mardi Gras was very exciting. Witches, Draculas, nursery rhyme characters and punk rockers thronged the street. King Kong stood on top of the World Trade Centre banging his chest and roaring, as a drunken Pope John Paul II was led away by the Halifax police.

On the corner of Grafton Street Elvis Presley sang, *Love Me Tender*.

"We should have put on our costumes," Megan said. "I feel naked."

As we continued walking up the street, we saw Frankenstein sitting alone by the side of a building, holding a large bottle of gin. We sat beside him.

Cindy took four cans of coke and the rest of the rum out of her large purse. We opened our cans, took a couple of mouthfuls then poured in rum. "I'll show Mom what it's like to get drunk," I told myself.

Sitting drearily on the sidewalk, watching the other girls dance, I was startled by a familiar voice.

"Kyla, I thought it was you."

It was nosey Mrs. Noseworthy from across the

street. She was so close to me I could smell the lavender toilet water she always splashes on.

"Where are your parents, dear?" she asked, in the syrupy sweet voice she uses when she talks to kids.

"We're with Cindy's parents. They're over there." Megan pointed vaguely up the street, sounding out of breath.

"Well, Megan, I certainly didn't expect to find you here." She looked disapprovingly at Frankenstein and at the girls dancing in the street.

"I'm surprised to see you here, too, Mrs. Noseworthy," Megan replied sassily.

"I was down here at the church getting things ready for tomorrow," she answered primly. "You do remember our special communion service?"

"Yes, of course, Mrs. Noseworthy. I'm taking part in it."

"Well, dear, you take care."

Megan watched the old lady walk away, then sighed loudly.

"Phew, that was close. I hope she didn't smell the booze. If my Dad gets wind of this, I'm in *big* trouble. She'll probably tell him anyhow. Mrs. Noseworthy doesn't approve of Mardi Gras or

Hallowe'en—or anything that's fun."

Megan went off to dance again and I had found that I had finished more than half the can of cola and rum. I poured the last inch of rum left in the bottle into my pop can. It tasted strong and bitter, but I managed to drink it.

Then everything went blank. I felt I was the only person on earth, and all I was aware of was the nice feeling the drink gave me. "So this is how Mom feels," I thought, just before I threw up all over Frankenstein.

The next thing I remember was Dinah and Megan each taking one of my arms.

"We've got to get her home," I heard Dinah say.

By the time we reached Dinah's house, I was a little better. "I love you all," I told them over and over.

"Shh!" Dinah whispered. "You'll wake my parents. We're going in through the basement door."

Long after I had gotten into my sleeping bag, the room kept spinning—like the never-ending ride on the Tilt-a-Whirl at the Midway. Every time I closed my eyes it started up again.

Hours later, I awoke with a pounding headache

and nausea and I felt as if someone had stabbed my eyeballs with tooth picks. I had never been so thirsty in all my life. My tongue was one large fuzz ball. Legs quivering, I made my way to the bathroom. When I turned on the switch, the light blinded me and my eyes hurt so much I couldn't see. Quickly, I switched it off again.

I couldn't throw up although I wanted to, so I drank what seemed to be a gallon of water and went back to the room.

Snuggling down inside my sleeping bag, I tried not to think about everything that had happened last night.

"Why does Mom keep doing it?" I asked myself before I drifted back to sleep. "Does she like being sick?"

8
Hallowe'en Night

On Monday morning when Megan, Dinah and I saw Mr. T. in the corridor, we couldn't help laughing. He gave us a very strange look. "Something funny, girls?"

"No, Sir," Megan said, trying to keep a straight face.

"It's a joke Kyla told us," Dinah added.

"Perhaps Kyla wouldn't mind sharing her joke with me sometime?"

"No, Sir. I mean yes, Sir. I mean...." I gave Dinah a dirty look. "What did you have to go and say that for?" I asked, when Mr. T. was out of earshot.

During recess I showed Mr. T.'s letter to Lorna, but I didn't tell her that some of the other girls and I had planned to go to the Candlelight Restaurant the next night.

Lorna showed no interest in the letter. "We might be moving," she told me. Her eyes were red-rimmed as if she had been crying. "The owner of the building came by last night and told my mother we have to get out."

"Where will you go?"

She shrugged. "Don't know yet—probably Dartmouth."

"That's rough," I told her, although I couldn't really see what the big deal was. If I were her, I would be more than glad to get out of a dump like that.

"Kyla?" I heard Megan calling me from across the yard.

"See you later," I said to Lorna, then ran to meet Megan.

"What were you doing talking to Raggedy Ann?" she asked.

"Nothing." I looked back to where Lorna stood in the centre of the playground, her head hanging down like a rejected puppy.

"About tomorrow night—we could come by your house at around … say ten to seven?"

"That'll be fine," I replied. "I'll wait for you on the veranda."

"Cindy can't make it," Megan added. "It'll be just the three of us."

The bell rang and, as we walked toward the school, I had a funny feeling in the pit of my stomach. I wished I hadn't used my address on the letter. What if Mr. T. found out I was the one who wrote it, or worse, what if he came to the house to meet Maureen? I was already in enough trouble. How did I get myself into these messes?

On Tuesday, we had a costume party at school. I wore a witch's outfit with a pointed hat. My face was covered with a white cream, and my fingernails were painted black. "You look real spooky, Kyla," Andrea said, when she saw me. She looked spooky herself dressed as the Bride of Dracula.

Everyone came to school that day in costume. Dinah, dressed as a clown, wore a green wig and her costume had large red buttons and bright orange flowers.

Kevin Clark took the prize for best costume. He came as a cigarette butt, a costume he had made himself. Everyone thought the prize would go to Megan who was dressed as Anne of Green Gables. Her costume was handmade, and it cost nearly fifty dollars just for the material.

After supper Julie and I took Bunny trick-or-treating while Dad worked late at the office as usual. Mom was in bed with one of her migraine headaches, but at least she wasn't drunk. I had enough on my mind as it was.

A pale yellow moon hung low in the sky as we walked up and down the streets knocking on doors. Hallowe'en is my favorite time of year and I love everything—from the ghosts and goblins that decorate windows to the Jack O'Lanterns that leer from verandas. Bunny, looking cute in the Red Riding Hood costume Dad had rented for her, held tightly to my hand. She was scared of just about everything, especially people in costumes and masks.

After the first half hour, I began to grow anxious. What if Megan and Dinah showed up and we weren't at home? What would they think if they saw all the lights out and nobody there to hand out treats? Besides, we were suppose to be in front of the restaurant by 7:00 in case Mr. T. showed up early.

"Don't you think we should be heading back now?" I asked Julie. Bunny's treat bag was already half filled with chips, candy, cookies and chocolate bars.

"We'll go back down on this side," she said, crossing the street.

Dinah and Megan were already sitting on the veranda waiting for me when we got home. "It's already five minutes past seven," Megan said coldly.

"We had to take Bunny out trick-or-treating," I told her. Sometimes Megan can be so unreasonable.

"Well, we'd better hurry," she said.

"Don't you want treats, girls?" Julie had put the treat bag on the steps and was opening the door.

"No, thanks, we're in a hurry," said Dinah, politely.

"The restaurant will be closed by the time we get there," Megan grumbled.

"Don't mind Megan," Dinah said. "She's cranky because she lost her bracelet."

"Oh, Megan," I said, "not that silver bracelet with your name engraved on it? What happened to it?" Megan was very proud of the bracelet which had been a gift from her grandfather.

"Who knows? It's getting so that you can't put anything down at school anymore. I'm sick and tired of people stealing everything in sight."

The theft problem at school was getting worse, and on one occasion the Halifax police had been called in to question a number of people. Things were taken not only from the students, but from the teachers as well. Ms. Cox, our science teacher, had lost a silk scarf and another teacher's purse was stolen.

By the time we got to the restaurant it was nearly 7:20.

"Mr. T. has probably already gone inside," Megan said. "Why don't we go in and order something?"

"I only have a dollar," Dinah said.

"I didn't bring any money," I added. Even if I had, I couldn't see myself going into that fancy restaurant dressed as a witch. Besides, it would probably take a year's allowance for just one meal.

"Well, I'm going in," Megan decided. "I have to use the bathroom."

For the next ten minutes, we waited anxiously for her to return. We glanced through the window, but it was too dark to see anything.

"He's not here yet," she said, when she finally came out.

"But on the letter he said 7:30. Maybe he's not coming." I tried to hide the disappointment I felt. Another anxious thought crossed my mind—what if Mr. T. had gone to my house instead? He had Maureen O'Riley's address.

"Maybe he's just late," Dinah said.

We waited for another fifteen minutes and Dinah went inside to go to the bathroom.

Moments later, a waitress opened the door and called to us. "Come on in, girls." She sounded very pleasant.

Puzzled, we followed her into the restaurant. "My cousin," Dinah whispered when we were inside.

"Who are your friends, Dinah?" the waitress asked.

"This is Megan and Kyla...."

"Ah, trick-or-treaters." She was interrupted by a tall dark haired man who came from behind the counter. "Maria, come see."

An attractive woman with long, dark hair appeared. After exchanging a few words in Italian, the woman laughed, then looked us over like we were on display in a museum. "Oh, Gino, they're cute," she said.

I wished they would stop making such a fuss over us. If Mr. T. were to walk in, he would be sure to notice us.

"Paulette," the man said to the waitress, "get them some sodas."

"Come on, girls," he said, leading us to an empty table near the window.

"You didn't tell us your cousin worked here," I accused Dinah as soon as we were seated.

"I didn't know this was the restaurant where she worked."

"He's over there," Megan whispered. "Don't look now."

I looked anyway. He was sitting not that far away from us, with a rose and an opened bottle of wine on the table. He must have been there all along.

Paulette brought our pop, then went over to his table. "Would you like to order now, sir?" she asked.

"I'll wait a little while longer," Mr. T. said, as he glanced at his watch and then poured himself a glass of wine.

We watched him for about twenty minutes. Every time the door opened, he looked anxiously toward it. He kept glancing at his watch and once he got up, went over to the window and stood there staring out at the traffic.

I was starting to feel as awful as I had yesterday when I had left Lorna standing in the middle of the school yard by herself.

"We sure put one over on him," Megan said when we were outside. Mr. T. was still sitting alone at his table when we left.

I agreed, but I didn't feel very good about it. That night I tossed and turned, thinking about Mr. T. sitting all alone in the restaurant with his wine and his rose. I kept seeing his face as he glanced anxiously at his watch.

I knew now he wouldn't come to my house. He wouldn't want to be humiliated twice by Maureen O'Riley.

It was a long time before I finally fell asleep.

9
A Meeting With
Reverend Kushner

When I got home from school the next day, Dad was waiting for me. He was sitting on the edge of the sofa in the livingroom and I knew something was wrong by the way he kept running his fingers through his hair.

"Mom?" I said. My heart jumped. "Is something wrong with Mom?"

"No, Kyla. Your mother is fine. She's out shopping."

I was filled with relief, but only for a moment. Mr. T. must have called about the letter after all. Now I was in big trouble. Dad went into the kitchen and came back with a glass of orange juice. He cleared his throat and shifted about on the sofa before saying anything.

"Were you drinking, Kyla?" he said finally.

So that was it. I hung my head. "Why do you ask?"

"I got a call at work from the Reverend Kushner."

"It was the first time I ever touched the stuff." My voice was a plea. "Honest Dad."

"What were you doing downtown at the Mardi Gras?"

"I was at Dinah's slumber party. I didn't want to go out, but everyone else was going. What could I do?" I knew I was whining, but I couldn't help myself.

Dad got angry then. He doesn't get angry very often, and it surprised me.

"You could very well have stayed behind. That's a poor excuse if I ever heard one." He raised his voice. "I don't ever want to hear of anything like this again. Do you understand me?"

"Why don't you say that to Mom?" I shot back. "Mom was so drunk she passed out in the drugstore. Why is it wrong for me to drink and not for her?"

Dad's eyes were wide. He opened his mouth, then closed it again.

"You don't care anyway. You're never around when we need you. You're worse than Mom."

A hurt look crossed his face, and I thought he might cry. I grabbed my jacket and ran outside.

When I returned to the house, he had gone back to work. I thought that was the end of the discussion about my drinking, but the Reverend Kushner called all the parents and invited them to his house for a meeting. We kids had to go along as well.

Dad barely spoke to me on the way to Megan's house. His mouth was drawn tightly together and his whole body was as stiff as if he had been made of cardboard.

When we arrived, Dinah and her parents were already there.

Cindy and her parents were not there as they were out of town for the week. Reverend Kushner said he planned to talk to them later.

"The grownups will meet first, then we'll call in the children." Reverend Kushner sounded really formal.

"Megan," he called up the stairs, "take the girls into the den."

"How did he find out?" Dinah asked, when we were alone.

Megan sighed. "Mrs. Nosewortly, of course, who else?"

"But how did she know we were drinking?" I asked.

Megan blushed. "Well ... er ... she didn't ... exactly."

"Well, how did your father know?"

Megan's face turned a deeper red. "Well, I ... I ... you see my dad has a way of getting people to talk. He always gets things out of me."

"You mean *you* told him," Dinah said.

"I'm scared to death of Dad, and when he asked me to tell him everything that happened, I sort of panicked." Megan lowered her voice. "He would have killed me if I had lied to him."

"Darn," I thought. "How could she? The dope."

We waited nearly fifteen minutes before being called into the living room. All eyes were on us as we walked into the room. We sat together, as far away from our parents as we could.

For a few moments, no one spoke and I could feel my stomach churning. Reverend Kushner, wearing his three piece suit, sat next to his wife. My dad, sitting at the other end of the room with the Taylors, kept running his fingers through his hair.

Mrs. Taylor, a very large woman who wore brightly colored clothes and a lot of jewellery, was usually very pleasant and laughed a lot. Today though, there was a scowl on her face and her dark eyes flashed with anger. Her husband sat next to her, his hands folded in his lap.

Dad was the first to speak. "Kyla, where did you get the rum? Did you take it from our house?"

"Wha....?" I was stunned.

"Megan told her father you brought rum to the party and put it in the other girls' pop."

I looked at Megan whose eyes were lowered. I tried to speak, but no words would come. I could only stare in open-mouthed disbelief.

"It was Cindy who brought the rum," Dinah said. "The rest of us didn't know she had it."

"I would never have let my child go to a party if I had known there was going to be alcohol in the house." Reverend Kushner's voice was oozing with self-righteousness. "The way the devil gets to people is through alcohol." His face turned red and he slammed his fist down on the coffee table as if it was a pulpit.

"No need to get carried away," Dad said.

"Where is your wife, Mr. Masters?" he asked. "Why isn't she here?"

"Never mind that," Dad said.

"It seems your daughter is a very troubled child,"

Reverend Kushner continued. "I'm afraid she's a bad influence on our Megan."

Dad curled and uncurled his fists, his face an ugly shade of red. "Now wait just one minute...."

I don't know what would have happened if Mr. Taylor hadn't butted in.

"OK, folks, this is getting us nowhere. We didn't come here to blame each other."

"I feel responsible," said Mrs. Taylor. "I had no idea the girls would sneak out like that. I have always trusted Dinah and I feel so disappointed that she has let us down."

I glanced sideways at Dinah who hung her head and bit her bottom lip.

"How do you feel about all of this, Mrs. Kushner?" Dinah's mother asked the minister's wife who had been sitting with her hands folded on her lap, not saying a word.

"I have to agree with my husband, of course."

Mrs. Taylor sighed. "I don't condone what those girls did," she said, "but what's done is done. I'll tell you one thing though, it's going to be a long time before Dinah has another party."

There seemed nothing else to say. When the Taylors went to get their coats and Dad followed,

I felt relieved.

As I was leaving, I shot Megan a dirty look. "The nerve," I whispered to Dinah, when we were outside.

That evening Dad came into my bedroom and sat on the edge of my bed.

"Kyla," he said. "I'm very concerned about you—and this drinking...." He spoke without anger and his voice sounded weary and defeated.

"I ... I'm not going to drink again," I said.

"You're sure?"

"Oh, Dad, it was just awful. I felt so sick afterwards that I never want to look at alcohol again."

"You promise?" His voice sounded sad.

I reached up and hugged him. "I promise."

10
Open House

The following week was open house at school and all day parents filed into classrooms to see their children's work. Even the corridor was full of displays. In my classroom the photography club had filled nearly every inch of wall space with photographs. I found it hard to sit at my desk and listen to the teacher while parents walked around talking to each other, but the purpose of the open house was to allow our parents to see us in our normal classroom settings.

I wondered how my sisters were doing. In the junior high they had been asked to write a children's book. Julie had drawn illustrations and designed a cover to go with hers. The primary kids had to make pictures of their families. Last night Bunny showed us her pictures of *Mommy asleep on the floor* and *Mommy throwing up in the toilet*.

"We can't let her put up those pictures," Julie had protested.

"Don't you like them, Julie?" Bunny's eyes filled with tears.

"I like the pictures you drew of Mommy eating her lunch better," Julie told her quietly.

Every time the door opened, I turned around in my desk.

Dad had promised that if he could get away from the office, he would come to see our work. Mom couldn't come because she was sick with some kind of virus.

I really wanted Dad to see the pictures I had on display, especially the one I had taken of Bunny in the attic. The other parents all stopped to look at this picture and found it *sweet*, *adorable*, or *cute*.

Jamie Foster's father, who owned a photography studio in town, looked at the photograph for a long time. "We spend a fortune on natural light," I heard him tell his wife, "and here we have it available to everyone." I was pleased that he liked my picture.

No one said anything about the picture I had taken of my family at the diningroom table. This one had become my favorite, and I had entered it in the photography contest.

"Look," I wanted to shout to the people who were walking by without so much as glancing at it, "this is my family. This is me, Julie, Bunny, Dad, and this lovely lady is my mom. See, she is smiling, she is happy and she is *not* drunk."

"Class," the teacher was saying, "the members of the photography club may meet Mr. Bryce in the darkroom." I knew he was talking to the parents as well as to students.

I was gathering up my things when Dinah tapped me on the shoulder. "I thought you said your mom was sick." I looked quickly toward the door. Oh no! There she was.

"She doesn't look too well," Dinah said. I could feel my stomach tighten. I was breathing in quick, short gasps and my knees felt as if they were buckling beneath me.

Mom's face was pale. She had red lipstick smeared on her chin, and had pulled her hair back carelessly in an elastic band. The brown dress she was wearing was about three sizes too large. I hadn't realized she had lost so much weight.

"They told me this was the photography display." Her voice was slurred and very loud.

"Kyla?" When she saw me, she came running toward me, bumping into a desk and knocking a pile of books onto the floor. "So where are all the great pictures your teacher keeps raving about?" I could smell alcohol on her breath as she spoke.

Most of the students and parents had gone to the darkroom, but those who remained saw everything. "Let's go home, Mom." I took her arm. My eyes filled with tears. When she pulled away from me, I ran out of the room and down the hallway toward Julie's classroom, so fast I almost bumped into Helen Clark—Kevin's mother.

"Something wrong, Kyla?" She looked concerned.

"My mother is drunk!"

11
The Alateen Meeting

On Wednesday evening, I stood at the end of the street waiting for Helen Clark's daughter, Sara, who was going to take me to a meeting.

Nearly a week had gone by since that dreadful day when my mother had arrived at school drunk. I still cringe whenever I think of it. It was worse than all my wildest nightmares and I thought I would never be able to face my friends again.

While I was in Helen's office, my mother had gone out into the corridor and thrown up. Later, when Helen helped me look for her, we found her in Bunny's classroom. Helen called a taxi and helped Julie and me get her outside. I heard one of the kids say, "Something's wrong with Kyla's mother." I wanted to run and hide.

Thank goodness for Helen. I don't know what I would have done without her. I stayed behind and talked with her for a long time, even after Julie had come back to pick up Bunny. It was dark when we finally walked home together.

"Does your mom get drunk often?" Helen had asked.

I wanted to say, "No, this is the first time."

"Yes, she gets drunk all the time," is what I did say, then I looked down at my sneakers.

Helen waited a couple of moments before speaking again. "Where is your father today?"

"He's at work. He spends all his time at the office and hardly ever comes home. His work is the most important thing in the world." As I spoke, I realized just how hurt and angry I was that my father hadn't shown up at the open house.

"What about your sister, Kyla? How does she feel about your mother's drinking?"

"Nothing bothers Julie. She is totally different from me—she's very cool."

Helen played with a large bow on the front of her blouse. She looked as if she was going to say something, but just nodded. "Does Julie go to Alateen?"

"Alateen?"

"It's a place where the teenage children of

alcoholics can get help. I'm going to let you in on a secret," she said. "My former husband is an alcoholic. My daughter, Sara, attends Alateen meetings, and has found them to be very helpful."

"Does Kevin go to the meetings too?" I was surprised that Helen would tell me those things about her family.

I already felt guilty that I had told her about Mom's drinking. Dad had told us over and over again that we must never tell outsiders what happens in our home.

"No, Kevin is too young," Helen replied. "You have to be at least thirteen. I'll tell you what, though. The next Alateen meeting is an open one and Sara is going to speak. If she takes you along, you could meet other children of alcoholics."

"But, Mom is not really an alcoholic," I told her. "I mean, she can stop whenever she wants. A couple of years ago, she stopped drinking for nearly six months."

Helen smiled at me. "Do you wish she wouldn't drink at all, Kyla?"

I nodded.

"Her drinking upsets you, doesn't it?"

"Yes."

"Why don't you give the meeting a try?" she suggested. "Perhaps you could invite your sister."

"I suppose it wouldn't hurt," I said. I was so grateful she understood me, that I probably would have gone along with anything she had suggested at that moment.

Now, as I stood on the street, stamping my feet in the chilly November weather, I wished I had never agreed to the meeting. I even considered going back home when I saw Sara coming toward me.

"Glad you could make it, Kyla," she said. There were two pink spots on her cheeks from the cold. Although Sara is about Julie's age, she looks younger. She has huge blue eyes and dark hair that is cut close to her head.

"Isn't Julie coming?" she asked, as we made our way to the church where the meeting was being held.

"She couldn't make it." I didn't tell her how mad Julie was because I was going to the meeting. She wanted Dad to make me stay home. "Honey, you do whatever makes you happy," was all Dad had said.

"This is it," Sara said. We were in front of a

large, brick church. "The meetings are held in the basement." As we walked inside, I felt knots in the pit of my stomach. I prayed that no one I knew would see me.

We were greeted at the door by a boy who looked about Sara's age. "Charlie, this is Kyla," Sara introduced us.

"Welcome," he said, holding out his hand.

There were about a dozen other kids in the room, all older than me, and all very friendly.

Soon a tall lady with curly red hair came in. She introduced herself as Anne.

"I'm a sponsor," she explained. "For those of you who are new, or are here as guests, the sponsor's job is to keep the meeting on track. The meetings, however, are run by the young people themselves. For the benefit of the new people, let's go around the room and introduce ourselves by our first names."

One by one each person gave their name. When it was my turn, I choked out my name in a hoarse whisper.

After the introductions, Sara got up to speak. "In Alateen we call alcoholism a family disease," she said, and picked up a child's mobile from a nearby table. The mobile had family figures—a mother, a father and some children. "Alcoholism affects the whole family," she continued. "If one family member is touched," she moved the mother figure, "the others have to re-adjust to regain a balance." I watched as all the other figures on the mobile moved.

"It affects us all," Sara went on. "As kids we all find different ways to deal with our problems. Some of us pretend the problem doesn't exist; some of us escape to the imaginary world of television or books; others deal with the problem by overeating."

I looked down at the green tiles on the floor. Whenever I was upset I turned to food. Was I dealing with my problems this way?

"I used to feel that people measured me by how good I could be," Sara continued. "I used to think that if I didn't get the best grades in school, my mother and father wouldn't love me." As she spoke, I saw some kids smiling and nodding.

"I no longer feel I have to prove anything," she concluded. "I have friends who know what I am going through, and I know it's very important to have someone to talk to." She looked directly at me. "Even if you aren't in an Alateen program there are people who are willing to talk and listen."

As I listened to Sara, I felt a sense of relief. For the first time in my life I felt I had found people who could understand what I was going through.

12
One Day At A Time

In the weeks that followed, Sara and I became good friends.

We called each other on the telephone and went out together. Through her I learned to detach myself from my mother's problem. Sara was like a big sister and I felt closer to her than I did to Julie. I have never been able to talk to my own sister.

One morning while we were standing in the school yard, Sara invited me to her Alateen Christmas party. "It's on Wednesday," she said. "If it's like last year's party, you'll have a lot of fun. It's not like our regular ... *ouch!*" Kevin had put an icicle up against her neck. "That Kevin, I'm gonna kill...." Sara's blue eyes narrowed as she frowned at her brother.

Kevin was chasing a girl around the yard who was shrieking at the top of her lungs, "Kevin, no...!"

Sara frowned again as she watched him. "Whenever things get too rough for Kevin, he cracks a joke or acts like a clown. Maybe it's his way of dealing with problems when he's hurting. He still feels that Dad let us all down."

"Kevin? Hurt? Gee, I didn't think...."

We were interrupted by Megan who came running across the yard. I had been angry with her since the day of the meeting at her house. I was really mad that she would bother me while Sara and I were having a serious conversation.

"Did you hear about Rags?" she asked. "Rags has been expelled from school because the teacher found her with Freddy Carter's pen."

"Are you serious?" I asked. She was talking about Lorna. I couldn't believe it.

"I knew it all along." There was triumph in Megan's voice as she spoke. "The whole family is no good. If they're not looking for handouts from the church, it's food from the food bank."

My cheeks burned with anger. "That's not exactly true," I said, but Megan didn't hear. She was running across the yard to tell someone else.

I couldn't concentrate on my school work that morning. Ms. Connors kept frowning at me from across the room as I wondered what it would be like to be poor. You could sometimes hide an alcoholic parent but, like a disfigurement, poverty was there for all the world to see.

It wasn't fair for Megan to say such mean things about Lorna's family. Her mother works twelve to fourteen hours a day at *Madame Benoit's*. Marie Benoit, who owns the restaurant, is a tall lady who wears black pant suits and smokes those long thin cigarettes that look like cigars. My dad said that she is "one tough cookie." He defended her once when she was being sued by a customer who got a bone stuck in his throat. According to dad, she's hardly ever at her restaurant. She spends most of the winter at her town house in Florida swimming and playing golf. I don't think it's fair that Lorna's mom does all the work while some other lady gets all the money.

Instead of going straight home for lunch, I went to see Lorna. She was babysitting, and one look at her face told me she had been crying.

"I didn't do it," she said, starting to cry again, her tears making dirty trails down her cheeks. "I found the pen in the yard during the lunch break yesterday and I was going to give it to Ms. Conners when I went back to school. I didn't take any of the other stuff. Honest."

"I believe you," I said, but felt hopeless and wished there was something more I could do for her.

"It's just not fair," I told Sara, as we walked to the Christmas party a couple of days later.

"A lot of things are unfair," Sara replied. Sara was so different from the other girls.

We were late getting to the party because it was my birthday and my family had prepared a special supper for me. Dad had picked up a bucket of chicken while Julie had baked a double layer chocolate cake. She gave me a new filter for my camera. Mom and Dad gave me a gold locket, and Bunny drew me a picture of a large cake with twelve candles.

When I walked into the church basement, the kids greeted me warmly. There was a table set up with cakes, donuts and cookies, and someone poured me a glass of fruit punch.

While we were singing Christmas carols, Sara came out of the kitchen carrying a birthday cake with candles. Everyone sang, *Happy Birthday, Dear Kyla*, and I felt my eyes filling with tears. "From your friends at Alateen," Sara said. While everyone clapped, she handed me a gaily wrapped present. I tore off the paper to find a diary on which was engraved *One Day At A Time*—a slogan from Alateen. Everyone had written their names on the inside cover.

"Thanks," I managed to choke. "I love it."

After sharing the cake, we all sat in a circle and promised to call each other over the holiday season. Christmas is the time of year when parents drink the most. I can't remember a Christmas when something bad didn't happen at our house.

"Try to stay out of your mom's way," was the advice Sara gave me on the way home that evening. "Have a nice Christmas no matter what happens."

13
Christmas Morning

On Christmas morning I awoke early, flung on my robe and dashed downstairs. Despite all the bad experiences I have had, I still look forward to Christmas morning.

Mom sat stiffly on the sofa in her robe, her face pale and pinched. When she saw me she managed a weak smile. I kissed her cheek.

Dad came into the room carrying a glass of orange juice for her. "Merry Christmas," he called to me. At that moment Bunny and Julie came bounding down the stairs.

"Did Santy Claws get in?" Bunny asked. She was terrified at the thought of a stranger entering our house.

"I have a surprise for everyone," Dad said, as we gathered around the tree. "Grandma and Grandpa are coming today instead of on Boxing

Day. They should be here by the time we're ready to eat dinner." The thought of seeing my grandparents delighted me.

It was a perfect Christmas morning. Flakes of snow like giant feathers drifted down onto the sidewalk, fell to the veranda and brushed against the window pane. Our large tree, dazzling with lights and ornaments, gave off a pleasant odor of pine. Dozens of gaily wrapped packages lay beneath the tree, and the aroma of turkey and dressing filled the house.

Despite all the coziness, I still felt as if something was not quite right, as if we were all waiting for something bad to happen. I think Dad must have felt the same thing.

"What we need is some Christmas music," he said, rubbing his hands together. "That ought to brighten things up." He looked through a pile of tapes near the stereo, and soon *Jingle Bell Rock* was blaring out of the speakers.

Minutes later we were so busy opening our gifts to each other that we forgot everything else. I received a pair of ice skates, books, a new dress, two new sweaters, and the CD player I had asked for. Dad had given all of us, including Mom, cross-country skis. It seemed like a lot of gifts but Dad always gives us a lot of presents at Christmas. Maybe it's his way of saying he's sorry for all the time he spends at the office.

Bunny gave me a painting of a Christmas tree turned over on its side. I winced as I remembered Mom getting drunk last year and falling into the tree.

Grandpa and Grandma arrived just before dinner, their arms filled with gifts. "Lovely," Grandma said, as she tore open the framed photograph I had given her. "It's beautiful, Kyla."

"You're quite the photographer," Grandpa told me. He had just opened a bottle of red wine and was pouring some into Mom's glass.

"It'll make me sick," Mom said.

"Not even for a toast, Sylvia?" Dad asked.

"Not today," she said.

I was glad she had refused. Sara once told me that for an alcoholic, like my mother, one drink is too many and a thousand is never enough.

Mom wasn't drinking or drunk, but she was still the centre of attention. She hardly touched her food; instead, with trembling hands, she cut her turkey and vegetables into tiny pieces.

"Sylvia, dear, you're not eating," Grandma fussed. "You don't look well. It looks as if you have lost weight. Are you taking proper care of yourself?"

"She hasn't been feelling well," Dad said. "Why don't you go upstairs, dear? Your mother and I will do the dishes."

Grandma and Grandpa stayed for four days and during that time Mom stayed sober. "I wish she'd get drunk and get it over with," I said to Julie, while we were washing dishes one evening.

Julie's face turned red with indignation. "You can't leave well enough alone, can you Kyla?"

Immediately, I felt sorry. Both Helen and Sara had told me it was best never to provoke anger.

"I didn't mean anything, really," I said. "It's just that I keep expecting her to get drunk again."

Julie narrowed her eyes at me. "If you behaved, Mom wouldn't have to get drunk."

Dad and Julie had told me this over and over again. A couple of months ago, I would have believed them, but the most important thing I had learned from Sara was that I am not the cause of my mother's drinking.

On New Year's Eve Mom and Dad were invited

to the Youngs' house. They were a new couple who had moved in up the street. "My wife is not feeling well," Dad said, when he answered the phone.

"Nonsense," Mom said. "I would love to meet our new neighbors."

Dad held his hand tightly over the mouth piece of the phone. "Are you sure you're up to it?" he asked, his face showing his concern.

Mom no longer got invited to parties on our street. The Wilsons who lived next door had invited her a couple of years ago, but she had passed out in their bathroom with the door locked and they'd had to call the fire department to get her out. The Scotts, our other neighbors, invited her over last Christmas and she had spilled her glass of wine on their Persian rug.

That evening Julie paced the floor and looked through the window.

"How about a game of checkers?" I suggested.

"I can't concentrate," she said.

"Look, if Mom wants to go out and get drunk, that's her problem. There's nothing we can do about it."

Later that evening, Sara called to invite me to

the Donut Shop with some of the other members of her Alateen group. I was so glad to get out of the house that I ran outside without my scarf and with my coat undone.

When I got there, Sara was sitting in a booth with Dawn, Sheila and Charlie. "How was everyone's Christmas?" I asked.

"I was shut outside the house on Christmas day," Charlie said grimly. "My father got mad because I put Alcoholics Anonymous pamphlets in his Christmas stocking."

Sara frowned. "Did you think putting A.A. literature in your dad's stocking was the right thing to do?"

"No, I can see now that it was stupid. It's just that so many of my friends' parents stopped drinking once they started attending A.A. meetings. I just wanted Dad to know there was a place he could get help."

I shivered, rubbing my arms, as I remembered how cold it had been on Christmas day. Poor Charlie.

"How was your Christmas?" I asked Sheila, turning to face her.

She played with her napkin before answering.

"Mom gave us her word she wouldn't drink this Christmas, but she did. She got drunk and forgot to defrost the turkey. Dad was so mad that he took me and my brothers over to my aunt's house and left Mom at home. I felt awful leaving her alone."

"Well," Charlie sighed, "it was her choice to get drunk and ruin dinner, wasn't it?"

"I know," Sheila said, "but I had hoped things would be different this year."

At that moment, the waitress signalled that our order was ready. For the next half hour we ate donuts and drank cups of steaming hot chocolate, laughed, told jokes and teased each other.

A middle-aged police officer smiled in our direction. "Ah, to be young and carefree again," he said to the waitress. Each of us fell silent after that.

I was almost home when I saw an ambulance pulling out of our driveway. The siren made a mournful cry as it picked up speed, its red light making eerie patterns on the white picket fences.

Trembling with fear I ran toward the house.

14
Julie's Secret

I turned the stiff, blank pages of my new diary slowly and carefully. It was six days into the new year, and still I had not written anything. Dad, Julie and Bunny had gone to Pleasant Park to try out their new skis. I was alone in my room. *January, A Time For Starting Over*, was written on the first page of the diary. I picked up my pen.

Dear Diary:

Mom is in the hospital. She got drunk on New Year's Eve, fell down the basement steps, broke her leg, and was taken to the hospital in an ambulance. Both Sara and her mother say this may turn into something good. Helen says it sometimes takes a crisis for someone to turn their life around. I don't know though. Sometimes I think Mom will never stop drinking.

Helen came to talk to my Dad about how Mom's drinking was affecting me. I didn't think he would speak to her, but they were together in his study for nearly twenty minutes. When she left, I heard him thank her for coming.

As I finished writing, I heard voices. The others were home from the park and stamping snow off their feet in the hallway. I put the diary under my pillow and went downstairs.

Julie and I helped Dad cook supper. Dad was quiet most of the evening, and I could tell he had something on his mind but it wasn't until I was ready for bed that I found out what was bothering him.

He came into my bedroom and sat on the edge of my bed. "I've decided to take Mrs. Clark's suggestion and try Al-Anon," he said.

"Dad, that's great!" I knew from talking to Sara that Al-Anon was an organization for relatives of alcoholics, just as Alateen was an organization for children of alcoholics.

"I talked with a social worker at the hospital yesterday," he went on. "Your mother is being sent to a place where alcoholics can get help. There will be people she can talk with, and she will be attending Alcoholics Anonymous meetings. It will be a month or more before she can come home."

"Does Mom mind being sent to a place like that?"

"Your Mom is quite willing to give it a try," he said, smiling at me.

"Dad, I'm so happy," I said, as I reached up and kissed him.

On the way home from school the following week, I told Sara that Dad was going to try Al-Anon.

"Great," she said.

"But that's not the best news. Mom is in a recovery program."

Sara smiled. "I knew things would work out. I'm so happy for you." She squeezed my arm.

"I just wish we could do something about Julie. She doesn't think Mom needs help," I said.

"Don't worry." Sara reassured me, "things will come right for her too."

That day I was surprised to find Dad working in the living room.

"I've decided to spend more time at home," he told me. "I can work just as well here as at the office. All I need is my stapler and I'll be able to organize these papers." He pointed to a stack of papers on the coffee table. "You wouldn't have any idea what's happened to it, would you?"

"Julie had it last. I'll take a look in her room."

As I walked into my sister's neat bedroom, I couldn't help but compare it with my own. In my bedroom there were books and clothes all over the floor, the bed was unmade and candy wrappers, pop bottles and half eaten chocolate bars littered the bureau. In Julie's room, books were neatly stacked on shelves, her clothes hung on hangers in the closet, and her shoes were lined up in pairs against one wall. Combs, brushes and makeup were all in order on her vanity table, and her robe was tidily folded across her bed.

First I looked in her desk drawer. Paper clips, staples, erasers and elastic bands were all organized in little compartments with spaces for pens, pencils and notebooks. Imagine knowing exactly where everything is without having to spend hours searching.

The stapler wasn't in the desk, so I tried the two large drawers of her bureau. Sweaters, jeans, and blouses were all folded neatly in the top drawer. I felt guilty going through her things, but if Dad was going to work at home he needed his stapler.

Then I looked into the bottom drawer. It was

filled with cameras, lenses, books, scarves, and jewellery. Puzzled, I picked up one of the cameras: *Property of The Department of Education* was written on the case. I couldn't believe it. My sister didn't steal ... but then I found Megan's bracelet and Andrea's camera and lenses—and I knew....

I put the things back and quickly closed the drawer. My pulse was racing—just as if *I* had done something wrong. I went back downstairs.

"I can't find the stapler," I told Dad. Then I put on my coat and went outside to sit on the veranda steps. I couldn't understand it. My sister—a thief!

I stayed outside until Julie, with her mouth set in a grim line, came walking down the street. She had been sulking since Dad had begun attending the Al-Anon meetings.

I went after her into the house, then waited in the hallway while she took off her coat and boots. Without saying a word, I followed her into her bedroom. She turned around quickly, frowned, and gave me a "What do you want?" look.

"I came up here today to get Dad's stapler," I said.

She reached inside a little plastic basket on her book shelf. "Here."

"I didn't think of looking there," I told her. "I looked in your bureau drawers. That drawer right there." I deliberately pointed to where she had hidden the stolen goods.

Julie's face turned red with anger. "You have no right to be going through my things." For a moment I thought she was going to start yelling at me, but she did something very strange—something I had never seen her do before. She sank down on the bed, covered her face with her hands, and sobbed.

"Don't tell Daddy," she said. "He won't love me anymore if he finds out what I did."

Suddenly, I felt frightened. She sounded like a little girl—no older than Bunny. She looked so bewildered and so vulnerable, I wanted to put my arms around her and protect her. But I could only stare.

She sat on her bed, curled her arms around her knees and began rocking back and forth. "Oh, Kyla. Please don't tell him ... please don't," she pleaded.

I nodded, then I thought of Lorna and a large lump came into my throat. How was this ever going to come right?

As I lay in bed that evening, I remembered what

Sara had said when I had attended that first Alateen meeting. She felt people could only love and accept her if she did her best. Was this how Julie felt? Did she feel that she could be loved only if she was perfect all the time?

I buried my face in my pillow and cried. We were like the cardboard cutouts on the mobile Sara had brought to that meeting. In different ways, my mother's alcoholism had affected all of us. No one had escaped.

15
The Apology

The day before Mom came home from the hospital, Julie decided herself to return the things she had stolen although she never did tell us why she took them. She didn't use any of the things—not even the camera. She just kept them in her desk drawer. Dad was very upset, but I think he was more afraid of how Mom would react.

My mother took the news rather calmly. "My poor Julie," was all she said. I was a little annoyed. It was never "poor Kyla" when I did anything wrong. But Mom had changed. For one thing she didn't make a lot of promises the way she had the other times she had given up drinking.

That evening she blamed herself for what Julie had done. "If I hadn't put too much responsibility on your shoulders, this would never have happened," she told her, with tears in her eyes.

"You've never had time for friends or time to lead a normal life."

She apologized to me too. "Kyla, I realize all the trouble you got into at school was because of my drinking. I'm really sorry and hope that you will be able to forgive me."

She promised Dad she would do her best to be a better companion. "I'm sorry I've made your life miserable," she said. "It's no wonder you stayed away from home so much. I hope that I will be able to make it up to you."

Dad reached for her hand.

His eyes were misted over just like when he comes in from skiing.

I felt very proud of my mother. I could see her being a sponsor for Alateen like Anne, who was once an alcoholic.

"Well, at least we know you won't be drinking anymore," I said.

She looked down at her fingernails. "Kyla, one thing I can never promise is that I won't drink anymore."

"But...."

"I'm an alcoholic," she said. "I'll always be an alcoholic. Alcoholism is a disease. I can only promise that I will try my best not to drink anymore." She gave me a weak smile.

I looked at Dad. "That's right, Honey," he said, "but after all we've gone through, I'm sure we can handle our problems as they come."

"Well, I guess it would be kind of silly to worry about things before they happen," I replied.

Mom smiled at me. "Kyla, you've really grown."

"I've lost weight too." I pulled at the waistline of my jeans.

My mother smiled again, and I knew it wasn't just my height she was talking about.

Julie confessed on her own, and since she came from a *good* home, she wasn't expelled from school. Her case was handled by the Youth Alternative Society, which meant she didn't have to go to court. It was agreed that Julie's form of kleptomania was caused by stress—stress as a result of conditions at home. Of course, she had to give back the things she had stolen, but because she had agreed to join Alateen, the case was settled. I think she only agreed to go to the Alateen meetings because the Youth Society suggested it.

What happened to Lorna seemed very unfair to me, but there was nothing I could do about it. At least Dad had insisted that Julie apologize to her.

I went with her to Lorna's house. She now lived in a small apartment building in Dartmouth where her mother collected the tenants' rent and cleaned the apartments in exchange for a free apartment.

Lorna looked surprised when she opened the door to us.

It was the first time I had gone to visit her since she had moved. Although the apartment was shabby and very cramped, it was much neater than the other place.

"My mother has a lot more time to spend at home," Lorna said as if she was reading my mind. "She goes out a couple of nights a week to take a business course through Canada Manpower, but at least she's home during the day."

She didn't say a word to Julie, just stared at her coldly.

"Lorna," Julie said, "I know you know that it was me who stole the things from school."

Lorna didn't answer, her mouth was set in a grim line. Julie choked back tears. "I know it was wrong to let you take the blame, and I should have said something at the time." At first, I had thought the only reason Julie came to apologize was because Dad had insisted but now, as I watched her, I knew she was genuinely sorry.

"So, how come you didn't?" Lorna replied.

"We were having a lot of problems in my family."
Lorna shrugged.

"I didn't mean to get you in trouble," Julie said.
"I really didn't mean to steal."

"So, why did you?" Lorna's voice was cold.

"We were having problems with my mother," I
said. "Julie didn't mean...."

"My mother was ... *is* an alcoholic," Julie said.
She picked at the little pieces of wool on her
sweater. "She just came home from a recovery
program."

"Gosh," Lorna said. She looked really surprised.

"I know that doesn't give me the right to go
around stealing things," Julie continued, "but I
was under a lot of stress."

Lorna nodded.

"I came here to apologize," Julie said, "and I
hope that you will forgive me."

"I guess it's OK," Lorna said. "It didn't really
hurt me any. I never liked that school much
anyhow."

Lorna didn't seem to be angry after Julie had
explained about Mom. She even invited us to stay
and listen to music. Julie declined, saying she had
to get home, but I stayed.

"I never thought your sister would be a thief," Lorna said, when we were alone. "She always seems so cool."

"One of the reasons Julie stole is because she doesn't have friends like I do."

"I know what that's like," Lorna said. "If it wasn't for you, I wouldn't have friends either."

"I'm glad you're my friend," I told her, and I meant it. I no longer cared what the other girls thought. "You can come over to my house anytime you want."

After the hearing with the Youth Alternative Society, Dad dropped by the school to talk to Mr. T. about Julie. He arrived just as Bunny and I were leaving for home. "I'll give you a ride home if you'll wait for me," he told us.

These days it seemed as if Julie and I had traded places. A couple of months ago I would have gloated over this, but now all I felt was pity for my sister.

We waited outside Mr. T.'s office for nearly fifteen minutes before I knocked on the door. "We're almost finished here, Honey," Dad said.

"Perhaps they would like to come inside and wait," Mr. T. suggested.

I hesistated. Even though I was only going to

wait for Dad, I could feel little flutters in the bottom of my stomach.

Mr. T. gestured toward an empty chair beside him. I sat down, pulling Bunny onto my lap. Then I saw it—the photograph of Aunt Veronica—on Mr. T.'s desk. He had it mounted in a little brass frame, the kind you buy at department stores on Dollar Days.

"Whew," I thought. "It's a good thing Dad is sitting across from Mr. T., and can't see this." But I wasn't going to take any chances.

With shaking hands I reached for the photograph, trying to hide it behind a stack of books on the desk. As I touched it, the frame fell face down, the glass rattling as it hit the desk.

Both Dad and Mr. T. stopped talking and looked at me.

Dad gave me a look that clearly told me he was annoyed. He picked up the photograph and placed it upright on the desk. For a moment he stared at it, a puzzled frown creasing his forehead.

I could feel my heart thumping, and my palms were sweating.

"A friend of mine," Mr. T. beamed.

Dad gave him a strange look, but said nothing.

"I have to pee," Bunny said.

"I'll take her," I said, more than glad to get out of there.

When we came out of the bathroom, Dad was waiting by the stairs. We walked to the car in silence.

Before he started up the engine, Dad turned to me and said, "Kyla, *what* is Aunt Veronica's picture doing on your principal's desk?"

"What picture?"

"Kyla, I want you to answer me. What was *my* sister's picture doing on that man's desk?" His voice was firm, almost severe.

"I ... we...." I began. Then I told him everything—about the ad in the newspaper, the letter I had written, even the trip to the restaurant. When I get nervous, I can't stop talking.

My father shook his head. The corners of his mouth began to twitch, then he threw back his head and started laughing. It was the first time I had heard him laugh in months; soon I joined in, then Bunny.

Dad just shook his head. "Oh, my," he said, "I don't know what I'm going to do with you."

"Oh, my," Bunny echoed, "don't know what I'm gonna do with you, Kyla."

16
Dear Diary: Things Are Working Out Fine

March 21

Dear Diary:

A lot has happened in the past couple of months. Julie has been in Alateen for six weeks now. At first she wouldn't talk at all in the meetings, but now, Sara says, she is starting to talk a little and make friends. Just last evening she brought home a couple of girls she had met at Alateen.

Mom finally got the cast off her leg. She attends A.A. meetings three times a week and Dad has become a member of Al-Anon. Helen Clark says the road back to recovery is never easy, but we are all on the right path.

Bunny hasn't wet her bed for nearly three weeks. Mom says her drinking was the cause of Bunny's bed wetting and that she needed a lot of attention that she was just not getting.

Mom hopes to go back to work soon, but just part

time until we all get settled. I asked her if she would be working as a real estate agent, but she said she's a lab technician and that she is going over to the hospital next week to see if she can get her old job back.

We do a lot of things as a family now. Last week we watched the judging of the photography contest at the Atlantic Mall. A girl from St. Bridget's school won both first and second prize.

Dinah Taylor took third prize and Kevin Clark got an honorary mention. When Kevin went to get his award, he walked on his hands. Everyone laughed, but I really didn't think it was all that funny.

Just before we left to go home, Mr. Bryce came over to talk to my mother and father. He seemed a little annoyed because of the picture I had entered in the contest. He said he was sure I could have won if I entered the one of Bunny asleep in the attic. I felt bad because Dad has often said how great Mr. Bryce is to give up so much of his free time for us.

But Mom just smiled and told him she was going to hang the picture of our family over the dining room table. It is her favorite—and mine.

On the way home, we stopped for ice cream. The waitress brought Bunny a little package of crayons and she drew a rainbow on my paper napkin.

The sun was trying to break through the clouds as we left the restaurant. It wasn't as grey and cold as it had been earlier. Dad said it looked as if it was going to be a nice day after all. He took Mom's arm, and Julie and I each took one of Bunny's hands. We walked the five blocks home together.